A Spiral of Being

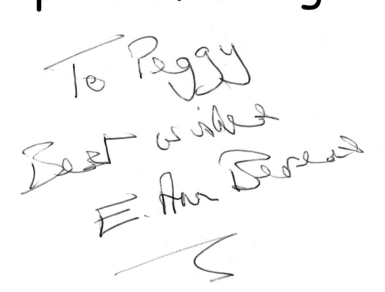

To Peggy
Best wishes
E. Ann Bernard

A Spiral of Being

E. Ann Berens

Copyright © 2011 by E. Ann Berens.

ISBN: Softcover   978-1-4568-4024-2
             Ebook   978-1-4568-4025-9

This book was printed in the United States of America.

To order additional copies of this book, contact:
Xlibris Corporation
1-888-795-4274
www.Xlibris.com
Orders@Xlibris.com
91242

REVIEWS

Ann Beren's poetry gives a depth charge to the spiritual quest. If you are on the journey, you've asked the same questions and waited for the words to come. Here they are, poetic, emotive, and filled with the wisdom of personal experience. May these poems guide you into places and spaces where you may wander to your heart's content, and emerge, refreshed and excited!

Rev. Patricia De Jong, First Congregational Church of Berkeley, CA.

Scanning Ann Berens' book of poems, A SPIRAL OF BEING, I felt a kinship with the author. In words the poet describes the physical or emotional aspects of the world around her. Her eyes observe exterior form. She explores the outer solid mass, gradually spiraling beyond the physical to discover a spiritual force—a manifestation of the sacred—beneath what is visible to the human eye. Her tone shifts to an inner understanding and accepting of how what is seen is only a covering for an inner invisible reality.

Many years ago, before I became a psychotherapist I had already experienced Carl Jung's belief that in wholeness opposites are reconciled; that one of life's tasks is to maintain, rather than erase, the tension between opposites; that Yang (the masculine driving force) and Yin (the gestating feminine force) need to co-exist side by side; that the Universe can only partially be known through tangible specifics. In Ann Berens' poems there is reflected a deep understanding of how nature provides healing for those who follow its spiraling below the surface.

Elizabeth Ratcliffe, M.A.—Retired Berkeley, CA.
psychotherapist based in Jungian theories.

CONTENTS

SECTION 3: BEING FRIENDS AND ACQUAINTANCES

SECTION 4: BEING IN COMMUNITY

SECTION 5: BEING AWARE OF EVENTS AND HAPPENINGS

SECTION 6: BEING ALIVE

SECTION 7: GLIMPSES OF BEING

For my husband Robin, and our children Carolyn and Keith
with love and thanks for
your constant encouragement and support!

Thanks to all those who have touched my life in such a way as to inspire me to write poems!
The love, encouragement and support that I have been given in the creation of A Spiral of Being is greatly appreciated.

I hope that this book will touch your hearts in your struggle to
Be your truest Self
as you were born to be.

FOREWORD

My story of becoming, and being, who I am.

A Spiral of Being is my story, through poetry, of discovering who I am, evolving, unfolding and coming to realize the inter-connectedness of all living things, my oneness with the Universe.

From time to time I have expressed my thoughts and feelings in free verse, finding it to be the best and most satisfying way to express my simple yet complex entity.

I want to share these poems as my way of fully being who I am, in the joy of connecting with others. Perhaps this is my part to play. For me it puts my experience of life into a Spiral of Being.

I hope it will spark you who read this work into becoming more conscious of being who you truly are.

SECTION 1

BEING WHO I AM

I AM

I am—
Free as a butterfly flying high—
knowing my place in the
Oneness of the Universe—
living my part with ease.

At other times—it's me—
unbalanced, out of line.
I struggle to be free, regain
that inner peace, tranquility.

I need some time alone—
to be—to focus on what's
really going on—let go,
pick up the thread and sew.

Life is a question—who am I?
I'm finding Who I Am—
centered on my Source,
sure of my course.

Let go of everything—loving
what is, living each moment—now—
not questioning, doubting,
fearful of the frightening.

No need to fear—everything
I need is here. Release, let go,
I know that I am free to be—just
listen to my inner guide—and hear.

CALLED TO BE

Created whole—a micro trinity.
I'm called to be my deepest self—
beyond the many selves I make.

Barely aware, I glimpse
through shrouded fogs,
beyond the maze of structures
built to serve my passing needs,
my wants, and see a blaze of beauty
like a sun, caressing everything.

Each misted ray of light filters
through walls and fences I have built
to guard my precious core within,
become an ever brightening radiance,
dispelling darkness everywhere
until no night remains.
I must let go of fear—let love and truth appear.

KNOW MYSELF

To know myself I must
have time to be alone
to think, to be, look
deep within—search
for my soul and know
that this is me.
Carving away veneer to
reach my inner core, I
focus energy upon an act
of creativity, drawing from
the depths within to find out
who I am—the way for me.

WHO AM I?

A cat, crouching in the grass, pounces
on defenseless mouse paralyzed with fear.
Driven instinctively to hunt, cat plays
his part in the balance of nature.
But where is my part?

Flowers turn their faces to the sky
attracting insects. Radiant colors set
off shades of green, lifting hearts of
passers by, playing their part in the grand
design. But what is mine?

A gaggling sound attracts the ear.
Looking up I see a flock of geese,
arrow-head of long necked birds
stretched across the sky-driven
toward a clime where they'll survive.

I watch with fascination, sharing
excitement in their freedom in a wider
world, while here am I on earth caught
in a pattern of life. Alone, I am a solitary soul,
searching for answers.

It seems the simplest acts give purpose
to my life. Sometimes I feel focused on a
beam—like an aircraft guided in to land safely
on a runway in a fog—not knowing
where I am, but listening in.

I follow what I know is true. I make mistakes
and try again. I learn, I grow, and slowly—
choice by choice, I glimpse the whole
integrity. But who am I to understand the
purpose of it all?

BEING

Search for identity, the 'who' I am, continues on.
I glimpse it in the shadow cast by an old oak tree
against a shingled wall-clear, dark shape, beautiful
—but when I reach to touch it there is no substance there.

I saw it once half buried in the sand of a forgotten
beach in Mexico. A shell—complete, unique,
exquisite shape, soft, gentle hues glistening in the
blazing summer heat.

I am, I have a destiny, a part to play. Incidental are
the eyes that see my course, that stop, distracted
from their own integrity, their inner life, to look, to stare,
compare, in turn distract again.

Each flower expresses glory far beyond its fragile form.
Here but for a day or so content to be. It is. It lives its life,
it dies. Its seeds survive, begin again creations joy.

I will to be the essence that I am—to glory in completion
of my task—to penetrate the clouds, illusions, dreams,
in truth to be the being I was born to be.

BEING NOW

Joy in the moment—being who I am.
How can I keep this sense of now?
Each breath I take is rich, sustaining life.

My eyes delight in what they see,
beauty in shapes and color surrounding me.
In sun and rain I wonder at each sparkling thing.

Energy within, bursts into action
in response to what is now. I reach
to know my oneness with the Universe.

Each present moment opens me to joy.
Released from clinging to the past
my mind dwells in my love of life.

Fully present in each instance guarantees
my life is real. I act spontaneously, true
to who I am from deep within.

WHO I AM?

Who I am is something different
from the roles I play. It's deep inside—
my essence, core, affecting everything
I do, the part of me that ventures far
beyond accepted possibilities.

Searching for truth, opening mind,
daring to examine new ideas,
depart from what's accepted
as reality—cracking the 'cosmic egg'.
Are we really bound by natural laws?

Is there a different layer of laws that few
have taught? Can we transcend the limits
we have learned, expand our thinking
through the mysteries of time? Must we
accept the status quo we know?

The roles I play in life, the what I am, leave
me confused. I'm mother, friend and lover,
daughter, sister, employer, other. But all the time
I am the same. Beneath these multiple facades
there hides a simple soul—the who I am,

My needs are small. I need to love, be loved.
I need a path to tread, a way to go, a purpose
to fulfill, time to express, reveal my inner thoughts,
and share them with humanity, fulfill my need to grow
—being 'Who I Am'.

I AM WHAT I AM

I am what I am.
I am here right now.
I am.

Let go of the dramas,
the fears, the scams.
I am right here now.

I am what I am,
my essence, my core
is one with the Universe.

Let go of the roles I play,
troubles that keep me awake.

I am who I am with
my unique way, my potential
to be the whole of me.

Let go of the limits
that keep me at bay.
Just be who I am.

Forget the distractions that
lead me astray. Stay on course
fulfill my way.

I can choose to be me
to be totally free—I live joy,
live love, I am me!

LONELY BEACH

I picked up a stone on a lonely beach.
It was smooth like an infant's cheek,
polished by tumbling ocean rocks
and the pounding waves.

I climbed an ancient, fallen tree
and stroked its sea-worn burl.
It felt like an old man's brow
stretched over bone.

I could stay all day on this lonely beach
searching for treasures to keep,
but the pull of the world was strong
and deep like the tide to the moon.

CARING

Caring—sharing gladness, feeling
another's sadness, grief.
Losing loneliness and solitude—
feeling vicariously.

The world is mine—its joys, its blessings, sorrows.
Even shared tears reap solace for the soul.
Escape from self to this larger whole,
linked with all humanity in one small
act of caring—belonging.

This, my way of caring—daring
to bare my innermost soul.

THE POOL

Cool, clear water creeping up
my sun-warmed legs as I
walk down the sloping sides
towards the dark deep below.
Painfully cold, until I take the
plunge, then feel a glowing
warmth work through me.

One with the water now,
deliciously caressed, no longer
fighting icy cold with body warmth.
A glowing compromise achieved
I revel in the new found state
enjoying the freedom of the
different element.

Responding to the flow with
forward thrust of fins no longer
webbed, but able to perform the
elemental task—propelling me, gliding,
floating, feeling the use of long
forgotten muscles, in my carefree
answer to the challenge of the pool.

I'm a multi-colored fish, undulating
lazily along, meandering between
water plants, seaweed and rocks.
Bubbles of air escape my nose
and mouth, slowly drifting to the
surface, until I follow them to breathe
the air again and land where I belong.

UNWELL

Limp am I, as flaccid as a lettuce leaf.
My crispness is used up, my body weak.
All I need is rest, the antibodies, hopefully
will do the rest.

Alone I lie upon my bed.
Each movement is an effort
and my muscles ache. I feel like
laundry washed, wrung out and laid to dry.

Things that seemed urgent must be set aside
like seeds of fruits lying dormant in the soil
until conditions are just right and germinating
season comes again.

If only I could turn a switch and pour reserves
to top my cup again to overflow, wipe out
germs, refresh, renew this vessel, to obey
again the dictates of its soul.

It seems a waste of time, but water must
be calmed and readjusted, fall in place upon
the surface of the land to find its level
now upon the sand.

HOW CAN I FIND MY PLACE?

Weeping in confusion on Mother Earth.
deflected from my path with doubts—
too many options open at each
cross-road of my life.
Hesitation leaves me torn, divided,
paralyzed with fears,
How can I find my place?

Beyond myself is order in the universe.
Inter-dependence among all living things,
fulfilling tasks instinctively performed for
which each is designed. Though unaware
of how they fit into the plan they add to
the constant flow of changing life, as
they play their part.

How can I find my place? Is it mine to choose?
Or must I submit to life, be blown by winds
of chance? I must find a goal beyond myself—
center myself on the Force controlling
harmony, the source of truth, reality of
scientific fact, until I am aligned—
in constant faith in this reality.

E. Ann Berens

WE ALL ARE ONE

It doesn't matter where I am.
You, God, are with me
in the mountains of BC
gazing over tree tops at distant,
higher, greened hillsides, staring
at a straight, tall pine reaching
to the sky, listening to tumbling
streams, bird calls, and silence.

I am surrounded and engulfed
by life. A gentle breeze sways trees.
Butterflies flutter over grasses—being.
And here am I, another entity
encapsulated in human form
but of the same stuff.
We all are one, infused
by the same vital energy.

I could be in the poorest ghetto,
breathing foul, industrial air, and you,
God, are there. I see you in the bright
eyes of children, in the courage of
those who dare to care. Even in
aggressive outbursts of rage, of those
who search to meet their needs
in the wrong places.

TRUST

Trust—like a wall of sand—built up in
warmth of human love and understanding,
grain by grain, tested and proved through chance
of mockery and ridicule, until a bond is sealed.

Solidified like dampened sand, trust takes
much building, but little to destroy.
Trust is a treasure of great worth. Perhaps
a jewel of the greatest worth on earth.

Freed in an atmosphere of trust
it's safe to open up, to share your
thoughts, to keep a confidence as
if one's own, like an unspoken secret.

A gap is bridged and understanding
is achieved if not agreement.
Honest questions aired lead to ideas,
a look at fresh alternatives.

Trust among friends frees
channels of communication,
keeps energies flowing through
the chain links of humanity.

DETOURS

Off track for a while—it doesn't hurt,
merely delays my goal, and that
needs contemplation.

Things I want to do, create and make,
must wait. The joy of doing them will
be intensified for waiting.

Time passes, dreams mature.
energy focuses for the consummation
of each task delayed.

There is a proper time for everything.

CAUGHT BETWEEN REALITIES

Caught between realities, unfocussed,
torn, unwilling to commit.
I hover like a humming bird from flower
to flower, never settling, just tasting.

Supreme creative energy—manifested
in all things—a force within, a light,
a way of harmony and peace.
I am a part of this, affecting everything.

Intuitively I know that this is true.
And yet, feeling remote, apart, I've learned
to shut the door, and feel alone and lost,
until a flood of light, of warmth, comes in.

It's like my door is opened to a garden filled
with flowers—giving their beauty to the
gloomy atmosphere.
Why do I ever close the door?

DREAM

Stark naked in a crowded room—
bare in a glare of light, no place
to hide. Alone and yet surrounded—
friends and loved ones seeming
not to notice me, oblivious of my agony.

Where can I turn? God, where are you?
I've searched for you in frail structures
made by man—defective, crumbling
systems of society. Are you truth
between questions and answers?

Are you reality permeating
natural things—exquisite beauty
in a single flower, strength and
stature of a tree, glow of morning
mist over a tranquil sea?

What is real and permanent?
What is sure? Mountains erupt,
spew ash and lava, solid earth shakes,
heaves, opens wide cracks, engulfs,
as if to answer our irresponsibility.

Nothing is sure, there must be more.
Who can I trust when those I see are
flawed like me? Suddenly I feel a glow.
My mind has cleared—the power
within I know.

CHILDHOOD MEMORIES

Thick trunk of tree standing among leaves
and yellow flowers, their stamens pointing
between waxy petals. I loved those flowers—
their perfect beauty held my gaze.

Rocking horse in a high room, place to play,
to dream, ride in a fantasy of danger,
alone, apart, lifted above reality,
lost in adventure.

Climbing trees with a friend, feeling brave,
shaming him, daring, taunting, making me feel
strong. Exploring the ditch beyond the fence,
peeking into other people's gardens, spying.

Then alone again, watching others playing
from my window. I, the youngest, confined to
rest, feeling deprived, but needing to calm down,
resisting the inevitable.

MARWOOD

Marwood—garden of utter bliss to me.
Growing reluctantly from childhood, plucked
from hard textures of a London suburb into
this belt of green, lush growth. quiet with
bird song among majestic trees.

Stone walls created hidden yards, sheltering fig
trees dripping purple fruit. Walled garden,
grassy walks led between apple trees.
Imagine such enchantment to a young and
eager mind, bursting from broken boredom
like a budding flower transplanted from a
crowded, smothered, arid bed, to space.

I wandered drinking beauty, sight and sound,
climbing trees, listening to birds and bees,
No-one made demands on me, they seemed
to know how starved I was for lazy hours,
and scenes like these.

Our London home had trees to climb, some
fruit to pick and flowers, but this was so much
more. Rabbits on dewy lawn at dawn.
Sheep crowding country lanes with Passmore
and his dog crossing to better fields.
Meeting with Mabel in her filthy barn, helping her
milk the cows, watching her make Devonshire cream.

A SINGLE THREAD

A singer, losing herself in the beauty
of the song she sings, becomes the song—
the voice searched for by the blend of
sounds—the song,

An artist, using his talent, finds himself,
the purpose of his life, expressing his
depths on canvas, finding an outlet for
his inner self,

I search for meaning in my life—it never ends.
No final answers come my way, just glimpses.
I'll never know the wholeness of it all,
the rest is faith and hope.

I'm just a finite part, a single thread in a cord,
perhaps a vital part of the whole. If one
thread breaks the cord is weakened,
so let me find my part to play.

I cannot know another's way or what his life
should be—only my own and that's not clear,
never plain for me to see. Each day unfolds,
each hour holds its mystery.

I follow what seems right for me, and as I lose
myself in the living of my life, so many
blessings fall my way. My life is full
and I know happiness.

E. Ann Berens

SPACE

Around each person is a psychic area,
sacrosanct ground on which no one
may tread. That space is theirs,
it must be recognized, respected.

Encounter groups sometimes lose
sight of this, destroy the boundary
set up to protect our weak defenses.
We cannot grow at one another's paces.

Time allows growth, but step by step,
as slowly as it needs to be.
Brick by brick the walls are built around us,
and brick by brick we take them down

'til we can see ourselves the way
we are, the way God made us,
meant us to be. So much we must
unlearn the truth to see.

BOLD INTENTIONS

Bold intentions this New Year!—
A network, like a spider web, of known
activities, catches creative thoughts
into visions of change.

Grateful for all I have—safe home,
a loving spouse, family, friends
and space to move, grow,
stretch into the flow of life.

Within my sight, surrounding me,
the world of chaos, war, despair,
shown on a screen—with the
flick of a switch—it's there.

I hold a place of sanity within this world,
keeping my space in harmony with what
is real. The seasons come and go,
wild winds and rain give way to sun.

I work for peace and order where and
when I can, believing there is meaning
in it all, that harmony is possible
in this troubled world.

SECTION 2

BEING CHILDREN, FAMILIES AND PARENTS

CHILD

I saw a face, so beautiful—
a child's—no more than six months old.
I could not take my eyes away.

It was a face of peace, serenity, tranquility.
The wide spaced eyes held wisdom in their depths.
His mouth, a perfect shape, gently upturned
close to a smile. Innocent, yet wise,
as if he was not new to earth.

Was this a Christ returned to earth?
I wondered at the sight.
What will become of him? Will he
know love and peace throughout
his life, as now? Or will he be
diverted from his inner path, his
purpose deeply known, and learn the
wily ways of man and lose his way?

Spirit—made manifest in flesh—
be strong, stay close to your Source
and be not led astray.

INNER DIRECTION

A child, a newborn infant
lying there—eyes searching,
legs kicking, absorbing every
sound and sight.

Given loving care and nourishment,
our child will watch and learn.
Clear examples teaching more
than words can tell.

As parents, teachers,
guides we watch, stay close,
provide a safe environment,
rich in diversity.

His inner nature will direct him
if he has the space to grow.
He'll gradually outgrow the limits
put in place to keep him safe.

We must be there, sensitive to
all his needs, giving him time
to think things through.
He'll learn from his mistakes.

That child, has more within
than we can see.
Respect his potentiality
and give him space to be.

NEWBORN

Her little apple, round and healthy.
Fresh fruit from her womb, gift of love.

Closed eyes, pink cheeks, not
yet open to the world. Just out from
the safe, close, warm, protected place.

A perfect form, no blemish, pure,
untouched, except by loving hands.

Round head, soft down, wide spaced
eyes. Miniature fingers, even finger nails,
like an unopened bud—beautiful.

DARCY

Gentle, gentle, softly, careful—
newborn child—like feather down
and dew and dandelion puff.
Newborn child, a rosebud—
small, compact, shawl wrapped
in sleep.

Little girl, protected, safe,
her features rest, complete
with budding bloom.

Waking, crying sweet female
sounds, she turns her head,
reaching for needed nourishment.

Newborn sucking nectar 'til
she needs no more, her dimpled cheek
fluttering butterfly smiles in sleep.

GRAEME

Sweet murmur of the infant lingers—
mind's eye sees him snuggled, cuddled,
suckling contentedly.

I hear his humming—shadowing our
talk and thought, softer than bees
on a Summer's day orchestrating
symphonies while soloists play.

An audible, primordial tone of
innocence—filters unwanted sound.
Listen to the soft hum of a nursing
child—the moment counts, eternally.

DARLING DADDY!

Little girl, safe in her father's arms
in the swimming pool, trusting.
Close, penetrating looks go back
and forth—shared with love.
Constant exchange of words and
glances like birds chattering.
Responses flow like water bubbling.

Father and daughter focused now,
no boredom lurking on his brow.
No pretence, no patronizing grunts,
but joy in the moment, laughter,
fun, daring her to grow, safe in his
aura secure in the knowledge of
"Darling Daddy taking care of me."

GRANDSON

New life laid in my out-stretched arms,
I look at him—he gazes back.
Distracted for a while, I turn away then
find his gaze still fixed on me.

He smiles and makes a sound—a hum.
We murmur back and forth connected
by an inner thread, like silver silk—invisible.
Gavin is two months old today. It's Christmas day.

This child, so small, such perfect form, open
to life, love, light—innocent—no past to cloud
his mind. Oblivious to time, his now is all.
He lies in peace, in trust.

Patterns of thought begin to shape his life.
Later he wakes to feed—urgent the need. Arms lift
him tenderly to suckle at his mother's breast as she
had done at mine. Early he knows the need she satisfies.

Pulling persistently he draws a thread of
liquid life from her to him, in symbiotic love.
Strong is the bond of father, son, as lying on
his father's chest, he sleeps again.

Then waking, plays—bounced in strong arms.
New life in older arms gazing again,
a different heart beat, different song,
then lulled to sleep again.

HE IS HIMSELF

Little boy—his tiny form
a frame, a fence for innocence,
exquisite energy, collected entity.

Barely beyond babyhood, he wakes,
climbs out of bed, slowly
criss-crossing arms and legs,
pondering his fledgling way.

Held high in loving arms—soundlessly
he yawns, rubbing his eyes.
Watching, he drinks the offered
juice, crunches some 'O's'.

"Hi-ee" he says, starting
a give and take of sounds,
meeting of eyes and minds as
sleep gives way to energy.

"Bru-ee" he squeals, neck craned
towards the window, searching for the
great black dog—his silent friend who
leaps, licks, loves, expresses joy in every move.

"Wat-ch" he commands with eager eyes
from mine to standing toy and back again.
"Wat-ch"—'til the toy leaps from the table top.
Reaching to catch it if we can—we laugh!

FATHERHOOD

Long hours of birthing done—
rubbing her aching back,
cooling her sweat-damp brow—
feeling the pain, the strain
vicariously—patiently waiting
while she labored on beyond
belief of possibility.

The final burst of supernatural
energy urged by his words, his faith,
she breaks the whorls from womb
to almost tomb, to life—the baby's
head explodes to air, his body
follows fast, slipping through—
caught in green sleeved, rubbered hands.

Laid on her emptied abdomen their
newborn son—alive!
Tears of astonishment, relief, while
gladness wells from bursting heart—
he takes the offered cutting tool.
Barely aware the implications of the
act—he cuts the vital cord.

Now father, mother, son—the new born
child—an entity, led to his mother's
breast—encircled in their arms.

PARENTING

If I did it all again I'd read more stories,
make a daily ritual from early times.
I'd sit my children on my knee cuddled
in closeness, love and trust, creating blissful now.
We'd safely let imagination roam, stretching our
minds to endless possibilities, far beyond
the realms of what is known.

We'd fly across the seas to sunny isles,
dive in the water's deeply churning foam,
bubbles bursting into clouds of air.

We'd ride together on a wave, feeling the rush,
the splash of salty seas. We'd laugh as we rode behind a
whale, sing as we coasted on an eagle's back on high.
We'd follow stars in endless space and know the joy
and freedom of our minds.

We'd dig the earth, plant seeds, smell rich,
brown soil, share hope, anticipation,
watch and wait. Each day we'd look for life to reappear.

We'd know the joy, excitement when at last
the seedlings forced their way above the soil.
We'd wonder at the mystery, tending it daily
'til at last its fruits appear.

We'd make a game of all the routine chores—
washing dishes standing on a chair, drying them
one by one, making a game like "pickup sticks"—
nothing must move but one. Sorting the knives
the forks and spoons, shelling peas and shucking
corn, matching socks and folding clothes.

We'd laugh, and sing, we'd share.
We'd hug a thank you, kiss away a tear.

AWAY

Our daughter's away in a neighboring land,
for the first time on her own.
Eighteen is young, but old enough
to feel you own the world.

She phoned today to say she'd like to stay.
Having a wonderful time—she said—no
more than that. She'd like to fly to
Santa Barbara, meet us there.

We turned her down. She must come home
as planned. She needed time, a day or two
to catch her breath, sort out her mind.
She tried to change our minds and then complied.

From child to adulthood she swings.
But soon we must let go. The pull of wills
is like a tug-of-war, the constant testing
of her strengths, 'til she is sure.

BE BRAVE

Look out through your eyes my child.
It's good to see through others' eyes
but hold your own.
Yours are the treasures that you own.
No one can know your needs as
well as you.
Search for your feelings deep within
and talk with them. Don't be afraid to fail
you will at times, like all of us.
Be brave, be free.

E. Ann Berens

HER QUEST

Some inner urge to find her path
drove her to fly to other lands,
be free to find her way.
She needed endless time, away from
too much stimuli. Distractions must
not interrupt her quest.
The fog must clear, confusion must give
way to calm, she must stand back,
detach herself to find the meaning in her life.

Leaving those who wanted much for her—
eager to offer help, to guide, advise,
she took her pack, her sleeping bag, a
minimum of clothes, some books to read,
a few necessities. Even her friends
were closing in on her. She went alone,
excitement for adventure overcame her fears.
She'd take it step by step, each day, by day,
open to endless possibilities.

The simple life was what she sought
to find tranquility, to reach green meadows
filled with flowers, the peace and harmony
she'd glimpsed from time to time.
Through lonely times, and joyful times with
new found friends, coping with ups and downs,
she grew in strength and learned to meet the
challenge of each moment as it came—the
ever-flowing meaning in her life.

THE PHONE CALL

Faint, familiar voice reaching,
linking us in present time.
So much to ask, learn, know.
Senses sharpened—awed by
distance and the speed of light.

Her letter reached us yesterday.
Eleven days from desert, over sea
and land. A flimsy aerogram marked
with signs designed to guide to one
small point on earth, across the globe.

Hearing her voice, so young, restored
our peace of mind. She traveled—eager
to test her strengths and learn the world.
Our trust and hopes were reinforced, and
mutual love was reaffirmed.

E. Ann Berens

PIP

Sister-mother, bonded deep through childhood—
teaching me to care, caring me to teach, to dare.

Away at school, from London bombs to Looe, a beach,
a banjo pier, close to Polperro's fishing fleets, with
seagull sounds and smells of fish and salty air.
Sister-mother Pip was always near anchoring my
fragile form, not strong, but frail and vulnerable.
Teaching me to care, caring me to teach, to dare.

Memories of growing up with Pip—
raspberries and cream one Saturday
at cousin Mabel's close to school.
Refusing me her cherry juice.
Walks on the beach, climbing rocks,
finding rose quartz and other precious stones.

Later she took me to a place I'd never been before,
opening my eyes to human suffering.
It was a humble London home.
Stale smell of urine in a darkened hall where
children played, a baby cried and we were there.
Teaching me to care, caring me to teach to dare.

We biked to Barnstaple, survived a noisy night, drunks
knocking on our hotel door. We were afraid, we prayed.
Teaching me to care, caring me to teach, to dare.

Each with our separate lives, but bonded close,
she went her way and I went mine.

A CHANCE TO FLY

They chose her after searching high and low.
   This little bean, once seen
they loved and took her as their own.
   Her eighteen months of life
had been a few months here,
   and there, moved from loving care
to loving care, but any bond was torn.
   Once born, she had no constant place
in which to grow, no face to know,
   until one day they chose her as their own.

Through all the churning years
   of growing up, the agony, concern,
for her, for them, for her again.
   The give and take, the joys, the toys,
the hurts, the limits set, restrictions broken, all
   it seemed just as a token.

But now it comes full circle.
   They gave her a chance to fly
and she has flown, grown to be a wife and
   mother, even now expecting another.
Secure, content, leaving no element
   of doubt and fear about her life.
But they are there, still loving her and hers.
   waiting to share, if she would dare.
The door stays open wide.

EAB

STRONG DYNAMICS

Strong dynamics work this family's life.
Connected to the wider world they
stretch and grow, each challenged,
nurtured, fed, led by their individual goals.

Safe in this wild environment—adventuring,
they grow their inner strengths, trusting
the Universe. Karate, dance, guitar and drum
express the beat, the throb of life.

Solid, yet flexible, their parents stand like
tall trees swaying in the breeze giving a
background of support, dependable, creating
harmony. These strong dynamics work.

REFLECTIONS OF A FAMILY GATHERING

Mangled, munched, emotions tossed
and turned in spiraled spasms of
extremes like waters crashing down
the falls from rock to rock converging,
forced through narrow channels over
jagged boulders worn smooth by
countless years of foaming, spray—
the power of cold, cascading waterfalls.
Emotions caught responding
to each vital human entity,
as feelings emerge, expressed
spontaneously—a never ending
stream to process through my
mind, to sift, select, discard,
retain, the meaning of it all.

RELUCTANT RELEASE

He left his yellow camping gear,
—symbols of security.
Impatient to be back with friends,
he left for Canada today, his
independent life, now clearly
marked, chosen from many
paths he could pursue.

Part of me longed to cling,
retain a thread, a web, to keep
in touch with him—my son,
flesh of my flesh, extension of myself,
yet separate—his own, not mine.

Slowly I released the string, and
finally, I pulled the line within,
became absorbed in projects of
my own. I freed him for himself.
Each to his own. I must contain a
focus on my own reality. I have my own
to care for here—they wait for me.

BE NOT A SHADOW

Be not a shadow in his light.
We act, we interact, the
overlap adds to the whole.

No hole is left unfilled.
Each vacuum, fed by
hungers, unidentified, but real.

Trust is a simple, loaded word.
Each of us has a path to tread,
led by an inner urge.

KEITH

He has come, come into fullness of
manhood—no doubts—he knows now
who he was born to be.

Alive, free, glorying in creativity,
energy focused on each moment
expressing his intent.

Flying down a mountainside—meeting
each curve, rock, block, no matter what,
careering, steering objectively.

Ideas bud, bursting into life like
Spring on a Winter's day, bearing
fruit in Summer time.

His search for constant love is brought
to completion with his chosen mate.
she with her children form an instant family.

She walks with grace about the place,
her head held high. Their newborn
child completes the ecstasy.

Life flows, overflows, like waterfalls—
merging, surging naturally.
They live on the keen edge of reality.

TO ROBIN WITH LOVE

When we met so long ago you turned to me,
and we both seemed to know that in each
other we would find ourselves.

Alone at first, in our own separate lives,
along the paths that fate had merged to
bring us to this point in time, we stopped,
we paused, suddenly alert, to find another
whose soul and mind seemed parallel to the other.

From that point on we grew to love, to
understand each other. We shared our dreams,
we planned a single life together. We lived, we
loved, we grew and each one found that it was true,
we found ourselves—each one through the other.

THE GIFT

He gave me a silver cross
hung on a silver chain—simple
and unobtrusive in design.
A perfect gift—symbol of
love shared over many years
of living, risking, doubting,
hoping, dreaming together
and yet separately.
His flash of insight caught,
in this one gift of cross and
chain, my search for truth,
reality, my love of beauty,
unadorned simplicity,
my faith.

FORTY YEARS—AND MORE!

You are the essence that I've always loved.
I want to live my life with you.
Accumulated tapes are gone,
we'll live each day anew.

No more assumptions stealing
surprises from the moment.
Gone are the fears, undue concerns
for me, and I for you.

We walk our unique paths,
sometimes merging like
streams converging—
to separate again.

Sacrosanct space is mine and yours.
Freedom to live creatively—these
are the gifts I have to give
as they are given to me.

You are who I've always loved.
I want to live my life with you.

FIFTY YEARS TOGETHER!

Fifty years of life with you—an awesome trip!
I've learned so much—you've helped
to make me strong.
Of course we've had our ups and downs,
and through it all—
you've helped to hone me to be me,
shed all pretense, know what I think
and what I want—find clarity.

We celebrate those fifty years
with love and gratitude.
Our life is good. We stand together
now—creating our reality.
Our choices lead us on to where
each wants to go.

We've etched a way of life that suits us both.
We love our home, a place of peace and
harmony. Each day brings challenges
and through it all—
we have the closeness and companionship,
a love that gives us space, support
and strength to follow paths fulfilling
our visions creatively.

I'm there for you and
you are there for me—
wherever we may go.
Sometimes together
sometimes separately, but
always loving, living supportively.

(Written for Robin Berens by his wife Ann for their 50th Golden wedding anniversary
September 22, 2006)

END OR BEGINNING?

He lay there still, just breathing
waiting to die. Ninety odd years
he's been around, active until these
last few days. He'd always been alert,
concerned with what he had in mind.
Dear man, I love him still, but I
won't hold him to this life with
prayers and anguish, no, he's had
enough, he waits to go.

Watching him fading day by day,
it seems like birth, subtle changes
happening slowly, but slowly.
He holds my hand, I know he knows
I'm there. Sometimes tears trickle
down his face, he looks so sad as if
he's loath to leave the ones he loves,
but knows he must. I share my tears
with his and find relief.

At birth we wait, a mother breathing
deep, urging her infant out into
the world. Nothing must hasten the
event. And so with death, it happens
in its own good time. All other things
are set aside, this is the only task in
mind, a loved one waiting close, just
being there is all he needs, his body
needs no fare.

Dying of old age naturally, was
beautiful. No pain, just peace in body,
soul and mind. Watching, waiting by
his side helped me be ready for his
end—or was it his beginning?

TO DENIS

Beloved family man—
ecstatic love radiating from his face—
that's how I remember him.

A bright intelligence, inspiring
his accomplishments, focusing
energy until each task was done—
building a family home, rejuvenating
Outward Bound deep in Zimbabwe's mountains—
Chimanimani—far from his motherland.
Creating a life—fresh start, supported,
nurtured, by his loving wife—
accepting the challenge of the wilds.

Beloved family man—
Why would you leave your comfort zone?
Dreamer, adventurer, extending love
beyond close family, to friends,
sharing the blessings of his life, fulfilling
mutual needs of those surrounding him.

Beloved family man—
with vital energy expressed on the
tennis court, playing the game enthusiastically,
he dreamed his dreams, fulfilled his life
and finally left with a parting smile,
a waive to those around him.

(In memory of Denis Lewis Berens 1923-2007)

DO ONE THING MORE

Do one thing more than you have set yourself,
break out beyond the confines of your mortal shell.
Be free in spirit and with vision let your mind
conceive the image of an action just beyond
the obvious possibilities. Imagination is the
means to dream—beyond the now.

Don't let discouragement dispel your dreams.
No new creation did evolve without a surge
of mind to overcome an obstacle.
Struggle to pass beyond accepted fact or
action, don't settle back in safety,
contented with a life of ease.

Those who achieve great things are those who
strive beyond necessity. Walk past the delicate
fences of security, risk more, live dangerously.
Perhaps they die too young, those who risk much,
living to the hilt of their existence, not stopping on
the brink of an adventure afraid to venture.

Look what they'd miss—the fullness of a
brimming life, its fruits reaching a ripeness,
bearing seeds of future deeds, adding their
achievements to the trail of trials and errors
that add up to progress, opening up a
richer life for all humanity.

Leisure to dream is vital to the human race,
without it life remains the same. Live on the verge
of vulnerability forever striving towards a goal.
Be open to surprises in your life, let serendipitous
events occur, those are the gems of life, refreshment
to the soul and mind, a chance to grow.

SECTION 3

BEING FRIENDS AND ACQUAINTANCES

CHRISTMAS PARTY AT MCKINLEY HOUSE

Just three years old—
staring at the Christmas tree.

Shyness forgotten, eyes focused
on an ornament—a little house
it's snowman standing on the porch
with two bright colored packages.

Lost in his fantasy, he stares in awe.
Freed at last to wonder, forgetting
all his fear, not clinging to his
mother any more.

Just free to wonder, stare in awe
and wonder.

EAB

DANCING CHILD

Dancing child—tumbling with joy
like an autumn leaf, at times a
wind blown dandelion seed caught
in a ray of sunlight, floating free.

Expression of God—new life, still
close to truth, no barriers built,
unfettered by fears, still free—
an acorn to become a tree.

Young child, new, sounds of
glee ringing from uncluttered mind,
clear as bells on a frosty night,
sparkling eyes mirroring love received.

The infant spirit newly clothed in
human form, an entity, holding
within an essence—perfect, pure.
Dancing child—completing the Trinity.

EAB

THE GATHERING

Friends gathered, sharing thoughts, ideas,
—in the warm sun, beside the pool.
Love, expressed by touch, a hug, laughter,
joy, delight in one another's being.

Intimate friendships, gained through countless
interchange in common search for truth,
for meaning, answers to endless questions
in our lives.—What's it all about?

Each launched on a path of discovery,
knowing our own direction, and in our searching
opening up to others. Energies flowing from one to
one in constant motion—exchange, response—

a ceaseless flow like water in the pool below,
wind blowing through trees, whispering
leaves, or like a ball tossed between people
in a carefree way—this ceaseless flow of being.

BLESSED FRIENDS

Marvel of committed minds, theirs
is a symbiotic match of calm
stability and searching intellect.

The height of joy, the depth of
grief, have sealed their closeness,
like solid rock in a tumultuous sea.

Triumphant through life's trials
they celebrate their anniversary,
nurtured by friends and family.

Balancing intelligence, responsibility,
with love and playfulness, they
look toward their future, blessed by God.

HELEN

She learned to trust the Universe,
to know her truth. A surfer poised,
she rides the elements—falling free
to tunnel through the waves, catching
each moment synchronously.

Her lucid mind commingles with
mankind, dancing a syncopating tune.
Through agonies of toil her soul has
carved her course. She walks a razor
edged reality connected to her Source.

EAB

MONICA

A stranger stood by the wall alone—
wrapped in a mix of shawls and
coats against the cold.

Her eyes glanced at mine then
looked away, down at the hardwood
floor, as if to say—the ground is all I trust.

I stood by the wall beside her, silently.
I waved to a friend across the hall,
another stopped to talk and then pass on.

I turned to her once again and said
"Were you in Berkeley when the earthquake
struck?" She shook her head again.

I drifted off to chat with friends then back
again, "I don't know your name".
She looked me in the eye this time.

"Monica"—she said.

EAB

JAN

Woman—standing tall with dignity,
beside her chosen man—
with head held high, crowned
with silvered symmetry.

Air of strength—born in the grassy
fields behind her childhood home,
riding wild horses, racing hills,
leaping logs—living dangerously.

Hot summer days filled with
adventure, moving free,
expressing joy, living, loving life,
unleashing energy.

Young voices echoing laughter,
clear excitement like waters
plunging through ravines and
crevices—hurtling to the sea.

Now—poised, she pours her passions
upon waiting canvases. Color, form
give vent to ecstasies, dreams and
inner mysteries, cycling creative energy.

E. Ann Berens

INTERPRETER OF TRUTH

True line of sight—
　　　from integrated mind through
　　　steady hand to paper forming
　　　shape in light, shade, tint,
　'til bees reveal their dance
　to human eye and high
　precision cars disclose
　their hidden mystery.

Love of life, of form,
　　　of shape and texture
　　　fired the fuel of his soul
　　　to excellence.
　Each task became a vital
　challenge to his intellect
　to learn, explore, discover
　truth in what he saw.

Environment of beauty
　　　set the stage. His home
　　　a sanctuary amid the rolling
　　　hills he loved to walk.
　Freed by the love of those
　surrounding him, his life
　evolved, exhibiting exquisite
　skill and inner peace.

(Written in memory of Richard Leech—artist, friend, who died suddenly in 1993).

JULIA

Poised beside the piano—radiant!
Contained vitality exudes
from every pore, like
a cat gathering energy
to spring.

With flashing eyes,
feet settled carefully,
hands placed on hips,
she waits to sing.
All eyes are drawn to Julia—
anticipating sound.

Her body aches to move.
Her voice surprises with
its strength and range.
She becomes the song.

Music overflows the room.
Vibrations—waves of energy—
explode, extend our consciousness
beyond ourselves, expressing
passion, life in all complexity.

LIZ IS!

Open to life and friendship!
Strong to conquer obstacles
and stay the course.

Liz is! She knows herself,
accepting all she is.
Being free to be—Liz is!

Joy in friendship shows
in honest, smiling eyes.
She understands, sees truth.

No falseness claims her actions, thoughts.
A sense of humor balances her life,
helps her to cope, to hope.

She knows her mind. It speaks to her.
True to herself, she listens, lives in
harmony with those she loves.

MICHAEL

Sunray could be your name!
Unquenchable, reflected light
dispelling darkness where you go.
Straight as an arrow, head
held high, a figure-dance
on ice, expressing joy,
crossing cold corridors of time.

Undaunted by the winds of
fate or chance, your courage
carries you through life
with grace and dignity.
Spirit of pioneers, adventurers
in time, your skate blades cut
across the universe in one true line.

ETHEL

Community of spirit—
yours is the company I seek.

Strong, lonely one—you stand
beside me close, holding me tight
against your side, earthing me to
ground while tears swell from my
eyes spilling my stress.

Eye holds brimming eye
in tender gaze, meeting the
moment's need for understanding.

Another speaks to me—while
I stand held, feeling your warmth,
your strength connecting me—
lifting downward thoughts—
reminding me I'm not alone.

You break your solitude in bridging
mine, all in a flash of meeting minds.

E. Ann Berens

LEONID

Look into your mother's face again,
trusting in open love, hearing her words
that soaked into your mind and gave you
wisdom, life, a vision of how things should be.
Those lessons learned remain.

Let go the memories of rage and hate
against the regime that you fought, with
heart and soul. Your courage, passion,
blazed your path through terror, agony.
Those days are gone.

Dark backdrop falls away, like a forgotten dream.
You've kept your passion, vision of how the
world should be. All yearn for peace and
honesty, true to our ancient memory, and
it can be. Each moment is a new reality.

Look into your mother's face again.
Reclaim the love and trust you learned.
See her in everyone you meet and live each
moment, unrelated to the nightmares of the past.
Your spirit lives, is free. Just be!

INVESTMENT OF SELF

Courage to involve our deeper layers,
in this battle for survival—not yours at first
but soon becoming entwined, enmeshed
unwittingly, caught in the sharing,
bearing of our souls.

Knowing the depth of your involvement
in our plight, seeing compassion in your eyes,
wondering why you persevere so long with us,
much as a father bears with stubborn child—
you suffered us.

We've learned so much from you,
shared so many things. Our minds have
met, have merged, funneling their energies.
Facing reality, examining our plight 'til
cleared of its excess.

Pared to reveal the naked truth, when
understood, decisions could be made.
Now it is time for us to stand alone.
You've suffered us so long, and we have
opened up ourselves in trust to you.

BECOMING

Daring vulnerability, they led the way.
Urging, merging to the growing edge.
Reaching beyond the safeness of the
known, trusting—on to new horizons,
sowing seeds in searching minds.

Shared visions of a world of love and
peace, own oneness with God's whole
creation. Leaders come, move on.
We learn, we grow—a constant flow
of life and light. Church stands strong
between two roads—bracing for disasters
yet unseen—symbol of community of faith.

(Written for—Ministers of The First Congregational Church of Berkeley, CA.)

WOMAN OF GOD

Woman of God, be strong,
know yourself and be alert, aware.
Be sensitive, responsive,
as a deep, clear pool of water
able to absorb the turbulence
that will trouble your waters
from time to time, wide enough to dissipate
the waves returning soon to calmness
to reflect the heavens again.

May the cool, wide waters of your soul
continually refresh and be refilled,
fed by the rains and rivers of God—
part of a constant flow of living water.
May no dam block its way.
Woman of God, stay open
to new ideas, new truths revealed,
new visions of eternity.
Acknowledge your human feelings
honestly, treasure them—
life is for living abundantly.

Chosen, yet brought to this time and place
by careful choosing of each step,
the pieces of your life have fallen into place.
Your spirit—free—has chosen well.
Courage to be, the strength to persevere
has brought you here, to this
community of mutual ministry,
to live, to love, to share the hopes, the fears,
the joys and sorrows of us all,
to help us open to a wider world.

(Written for the ordination of Diane Dulin as Assistant Minister to the First Congregational Church of Berkeley, CA.)

ENTELECHY

I saw God's grandeur in a human being.
Abundance flowed through every pore.
Larger than life she seemed, and yet
no more than you or I could be.

At times she is as earthy as the rest of us,
but far beyond the local self, she lives
from her essence or entelechy,
seeing the wholeness of the Universe.

Her voice, magnificent in depth
and tone, describes complexities—
global changes taking place; instant
communication through the internet;
melding of colored skins, no longer
white or black, but mingled, breaking
barriers of race and prejudice.

Her words come fast, opening minds
to widening possibilities, inspiring
positive results to dreams.
My mind expands as we dance and sing,
flexing our dormant parts to integrate
ourselves to focus, overcome our blocks,
stretching beyond all boundaries.

I join the flow of evolution as I grow and
know that what I will, will be.
I see my path with greater clarity,
helped by countless long-gone counselors.
I'll play my part, that's all I need to do,
knowing I'm not alone, but joined to all eternity.

SHARED LIVES

Rare gifts shared.
Moments of delight remembered,
time spent together on beaches—
watching waters rising, falling.

Days became years together,
leaping from highs to lows—
tsunami's surging waves to rippling,
gentle, lapping, shoreline tides.

Out of dichotomy a flower grew,
a child so full of joy—light of
your lives, proof of your love,
evidence of ecstasy.

Two gifted lives with different dreams,
matched in certain ways, yet far apart.
Torn between love and peace of mind,
reaching tangentially for unity.

E. Ann Berens

JENNY

A tree shook—
but there was no wind.

The air was still with peace,
beauty was everywhere—
in every blade of grass.
Each flower glowed with a
radiance of its own.
Birds sang, water bubbled by,
sparkling with reflected light.

Joy filled the scene—an air
of expectancy, excitement, hope.
Freedom of spirit pervades
the air, an energy released—
no longer bound within
confining, hurting walls—
But free!

(Written for Jenny Langner and read at her memorial service.)

FRIEND

What is it that makes a man so loved?
Is it his understanding that requires no words?
His look—inspiring confidence? Humanity
that links him one to one with others?

His humble, unassuming manner calls on our
common vulnerability. Our own unsearched,
and barely tapped, resources become available
raised by the faith we have in one another.

One man's insight of another man's potential
lends him, by telepathy, a vision and a hope.
The glimpsing of the power that is within gives
courage to attempt, to dare the seemingly impossible.

So many records have been broken by the urging
of a coach, a friend, a person who has faith,
imagination, sees in another as his brother,
possibilities surpassing his own ken.

Vision of achievement nourished by encouragement,
grows to be reality. A man is stretched beyond
his self-made limitations, putting out efforts
he has never made before.

A friend, the deepest kind of friend, is one who
shares the pains, despairs, the joys and hopes,
is there behind the scenes—a strength—supportive
when you need a friend to understand.

A friend is one who will not be afraid to speak the
truth, search his heart, express the way he feels.
His openness helps you determine what to do,
helps you to know the way that's right for you.

SECTION 4

BEING IN COMMUNITY

UNITED

Each from our diverse ways we
come separate in our solitary
search, our private quests, bringing
resources drawn from our experience.

Joined in our differences,
juxtaposed for strength,
entwined in common purpose
creating new wholeness.
Each warp and weft, woven
intricately into a functional
fabric of extraordinary hue.

Focused in spirit on a cosmic cause,
intent on a vision of a perfect world—
the blend of gifts, of energies, creates
a new reality which has no bounds.

THE TEAM

Weave of personalities, a warp and weft
born of a passion to erupt the status quo.
Shared vision of a better world—prisons evolving
into havens of healing in a world of woes.
Children drawn out of chaos into loving care,
peace and harmony, nurtured to living wholesomely.
Tension of close relationships weave a fabric
strong and true, working a common theme.
Each vision born—its own effect becomes
a catalyst for change.
Focused energy creates reality.
Don't stop there—just follow through!

TAPESTRY

We grow, we interweave our
lives, in unimagined tapestry.
Led by that inner energy,
expressing joy, knowing our way,
and only ours, until—a task complete,
threads cut and woven in—we glimpse
the beauty of the whole design and
wonder at our part in it.

Free to begin anew, spontaneous
life radiating from a knowledge of
at-one-ment with creation and with
God, new patterns form and overlap.
Each thread moves through, true
to its unique way, affecting everything.
Lost when alone, our colors
juxtaposed, bring each to life.

Our lives unite in common cause
enriching and enriched, then part again,
free in the purpose of our lives.
We must let go when living leads
us on from old to new in great
harmonious design—each of us
part of the tapestry—the wholeness
of eternity.

FREE SPIRITS

As fellow travelers wending
our separate ways—we step
with joy, excitement, in a freedom
of spirit that cannot be denied.
Living our lives spontaneously,
each one unique in every way,
our spirits dance—braced for surprise!

Joining our energies fleetingly,
healing, nurturing, learning,
blending our strengths, our
weaknesses, weaving a harmony,
a work of art, vivid in hue,
of diverse warp and weft—
unlike anything before.

Constant motion in the sea of life,
grasping for joy each moment
in its richness, aware of challenge,
each instant lost for ever if not met.
Vitality—fruit of the spirit—exploding
into life, like bushes bursting from the earth,
ablaze with blossoms in a garden lushly green.

Blessed are these sharings over years
or even days. Our paths cross briefly
weaving patterns with threads of life
affecting the universe unwittingly!
Free spirits all—poised in a subtle
balance with God's will, like the miracle
of a hovering humming bird!

JOYFUL SPIRIT

Joyful spirit focused.
Light on a prism diffused
to each member of the choir,
each instrument.

Radiant colors, part of a
glorious rainbow of sounds.
Music collected, conducted,
channeled through one and all.

Minds of musicians inspiring
sound, glinting from giant silver
mobiles hung from the vaulted
ceilings of the church at Christmas time.

Joy to the world—movement, dancing,
infectious joy displayed, transmitted
through, beyond, below, behind—
'til all our pulses beat as one.

EAB

CLEMATIS

Each day the clematis has grown,
reaching, curling leafy tentacles around
the wires upon the archway found.
Sun and rain, providing stimuli, excite its
growth. It must respond to these
and to the touch of objects in its path.

But we can hide, decide to live a sheltered
life, not venture out, avoid the risk of
vulnerability, surround ourselves with
people of like mind, a kind accepting of the
status quo. What empty lives—to lose the
challenge of humanity.

Life would become a bore, a chore, no stimuli
to force us to seek out resources deep within.
Our inner drive will keep us reaching out
not building walls around ourselves but
feeling, healing, hurting with the world.
We must take risks,

Stagnating we become as useless as a
weed, the seed within dries up and we remain
the same, a fraction of the person we could be.
The clematis grows round the arch enriching
the archway with its purple flowers, adding
to the peace and harmony.

CLOWN FACE

Clown face—mask of fun and laughter—stretching
minds to wonder, look outside, beyond, below, above,
inwards, outwards, everywhere. Gymnastics of the mind
squeezing a laugh, a tear, easing reluctant response,
raising a spirit, soaring to join the merriment, reaching
through sadness of young and old. Climbing huge steps
releasing effervescence from children's faces, putting
make-up on, touching, joining hands, linking in fun.

Cracking a door ajar, glimpsing a fearful heart,
with leaps and bounds over defending walls.
Sparking joy, to melt the hard-packed wall with
simple foolishness, bringing up deep sunk smiles
like bubbles bursting on the surface of a stagnant pool,
setting free some hidden mirth blended with anger,
hurt, long buried deep within—forgiving, healing.
Watering tight closed buds to open into radiant flowers.

Seeding laughter, lifting hearts with story, dance and song.
bringing hope to tired forgotten faces, holding hands.
Clown face—coaxing new wrinkles on old faces,
looking into lonely eyes, stroking brows starved of human
contact, arousing memories of distant friends, bringing
tears to dried up eyes, stirring spirits, oiling rusted springs.
Clown face—mask of fun and laughter, leaving a trail,
a reawakened glow within, like bright beads on a string,

FEAR

Fear is the foe we must defeat.
If fled, its power gains strength.
It grows like a monstrous weed,
expands, spreads like a flood
encroaching shores of sanity.

Faced in cold reality fear shrinks,
becomes a manageable thing.
Nightmares lose their terror.
Facts recognized for what they are,
bring thoughts to focus.

Courage is found to take a step
to counteract the fear. A vision,
dream, is not unreachable.
Intent, with effort and imagination,
can be reached.

LONELY

Young woman in a stark new house
searching for warmth in the heat of the day.
Cool in the beautiful barren rooms,
white walls, wood beams, brown
tiles around brown hearth, filled
with cut logs waiting for flame.

Clear picture windows not yet draped,
reveal a glowing world. Sun on trees
and rolling hills, homes in the distance
contrasting her loneliness within.

Large new house demanding color,
texture, form, to soften cold, bare, bounds.
Hollow shell of wood, waiting for life
and laughter, sounds of children's voices.
Only the wind sings high on this ridge.
above the reservoir, a valley either side.

Only the trees around the house,
old oaks saved with love and care,
give some security and promise
of summer shade.

Young woman, get out with friends
and have some fun. Revive your
orphaned spirit for a while.
Forget your cares, be not a captive
of your castle on the hill.

EAB

VOLUNTEER

His eyes were clear, they focused
kindly on the one with whom he spoke.
No cloud of inner turmoil deflected
his attention from the moment.

He had a look of wholeness, health.
Fun and laughter set his mouth.
Crows feet around his eyes
mellowed his steady gaze.

I wondered at what I read upon his face.
Instinctively I trusted him and knew that
there was much that I could learn from him.
No false assumptions would delay his understanding.

I asked him of his life. He saw himself a channel
for a force of life flowing through humanity.
Love was the key that set him free.
Love saw the human need.

Response released the power of love, was
blessed by it. The helper and the helped created
a triangle with God. He saw no strata in society.
All were equal channels for the force of love.

TO A BLIND FRIEND

Don't ask me why I cry.
Your penetrating questions
pierce my shield too fast,
leaving me speechless, struggling
with emotions roused by your search.

Three years without your sight—
trusting vulnerably, starting life again.
From being proud and strong—
ready to take the lead at every turn,
to letting someone help you in
your need. Not feeling weak, but
letting them be strong. Finding new
strengths within, replacing outer eye
with inner sight. Courage to be.

Inquiring mind—questioning, searching,
challenging every thought. Not seeing,
feeling all the way, leaving no stone unturned.
Being proud again, but in a different way,
finding, though blind, you have a lot to give, to say.

Those without eyes are led by those who see;
those without sound or speech rely on
friends to voice their thoughts, their needs;
the crippled, maimed—all make one body
of humanity, their inner purposes intensified,
undaunted by adversity.

THE WALL SITTERS

Why do you sit by the wall and stare?
Why don't you climb from you shell and tell?
Is your reality so dull, so dead?
Is there no hope that will lift your head?
Why should I wish that you'd move around?
Why can't I leave you to stay aground?

You know how to eat, to dress, to speak,
move out of danger, away from hurt.
You know what is happening, you want to survive.
What makes you hide away, alive?
What are the fears that wall you in,
prevent you from daring to try again?

Open your life, your potential is there.
You can choose to sit or to live and dare.
There are people who care just waiting to
share. Just think of your power!
Are you waiting for something in your life?
Can you listen again for that inner voice?

No one can force you to move around,
you can make new choices every hour,
decide what to wear, when to get up,
what you will eat and when to sleep.
Each decision you make, however small,
affects something else and makes you feel tall.

We all make mistakes, then we try again.
We know we are free to experience gladness,
we've all known despair, and shared joy
and sadness. We make our decisions,
soon feel in control, then—
we'll know that we're whole.

E. Ann Berens

JOAN'S WALL

She built a wall around her place.
She needed privacy and space.
It was a way to cope, to hope,
to keep herself from harm.

There was a time before she built her
wall when she was young and very
vulnerable. She was a sharp, bright
child who loved and trusted all.

Her days were filled with joy.
Excitement bubbled, senses reeled,
her overwhelming feelings scarce could
be contained within her whispy frame.

Too often in a day that started bright,
a scolding she'd provoke. Her spirits would
come crashing down, and leave her very low.
She'd crawl into her shell and hide.

She'd quieten down and stay confined and safe,
safe from the cruel world that crushed her
happiness, turning her love of life
to bitterness and hurt.

The wall began to grow. In anger she'd pick up
another brick and pile it on the one before.
Defiance to injustice, needs unmet for love,
companionship and sharing.

But now that she is grown and lives alone,
the wall she built so long ago is strong.
She's learned through many years of
struggle how to survive, be sane, remain the same.

But now it's not enough. She longs for closeness
to a friend on whom she can depend. Her fear is
great, how can she risk again the feelings that
were shattered when she was a child?

A curiosity, a yearning, dares her to take
away the wall. She looks outside to glimpse the
freedom for her soul. She watches people laughing,
sharing their joys and sorrows, both.

They're all together as a whole, linked by flowing
energies. Has she the strength she lacked when she was
young or will the waves of feelings sweep her under,
drown her in despair again?

She's learned to live behind her wall, safely,
learned to walk beyond the wall, only to return
and rest awhile. Each time she ventures out she stays
out longer, travels farther, risks a little more.

One day she'll join the human race
again and never more return
for refuge in the castle that
she built behind the wall.

THE DOERS

Why do we put upon so few
the lot to do the tasks we see
need doing? They are the chosen
ones, we say, the doers of the
will of God. We are just simple
followers, sheep, the helpless
millions searching deep for
some direction in our lives.

We look to them, the few we have
made leaders in our midst, putting
on them responsibilities that are our own.
We load them with our heavy burdens,
asking of them to lift them up to God.
The Holy Spirit, we say, will flow through
them to those in need—healing the sick,
comforting and strengthening the weak.

But we are wrong. We're all in this together.
The sun does not pick and choose who
will receive its warmth and light.
Water can flow through any channels.
Forces and energies surround us constantly,
with false humility we block them out.
God made us all to do his will,
within our own capacity.

Open us Lord and use us every one.
Flow through us with your power of love.
Forgive us for the way we block you out.
Take us the way we are. The power is
yours not ours. Help us to do our part
and share the work together. Each one,
a link in the human chain, may none of us
frustrate the chain reaction of your love.

THE CANDIDATE

I watched him closely as he walked the aisle,
searching for strengths and weaknesses.
We had a task to do this day. We must be sure
this was our man—endorse the Search
Committee's choice, reject, refuse, if there was
cause. He had these choices too.

I watched him closely as he sat in view.
I saw him whole, complete, rare smiles
revealed a confidence, acceptance
among men. Submissiveness was far
from him. Strong, outgoing, filled
with vitality—a family man.

No arrogance was there, just self respect.
No false humility reduced his strength.
He was together, living in the moment—now.
He knew himself, one who could lead us on,
whom we could trust to help us know God's
will for us? An answer to heartfelt prayer.

Awed by the outcome, our hopes surpassed,
our wavering faith restored, we were aware of
unknown purpose in the air. We must prepare.
Each has their part to play, unique, alone and
yet together, open to unknown possibilities
beyond our understanding.

E. Ann Berens

VENTURES IN VULNERABILITY

A scientist glimpses a new concept,
just as a flash of lightening reveals
the landscape for a second,
'til all is dark again.

That glimpse, that vision of truth,
reality perhaps, drives to research.
Testing, proving all scientific laws
accepted until now.
Checked against the new idea,
could there be one minute flaw
that could dissolve, prove wrong
accepted scientific law?

Man's search for truth leads him to
explore, endure a chance of failure.
Courage to challenge hitherto accepted
facts allows the cosmic egg to crack.
He's dared to open up his world, to
penetrate the bounds of his reality,
to break new ground, explore his vision
of the truth—venture of vulnerability.

A scientist must prove his case, and
if he's wrong, if all his searching leads
him back to where he was before,
he must accept that truth.
Examination of each law has
taught him much, and patiently he'll
start again from the tested, proven
rock of his reality.

COUNSELOR—BE WISE!

Counselor, be wise!
You cannot know it all.
God only knows the whole,
the truth, the all. Out of a
trillion cells new life begins,
a being delicately poised in
perfect harmony with all that is,
part of an integral design.

Counselor, be wise!
Each to his own responsibility.
Each act creates response, each
word, each sound adds to a chord.
Movement is constant, waters flow, vapors
rise, the earth vibrates and creatures bend
and blow, like breezes on a summer day.
Each smallest choice is ours to make.

May every act emerge from love, each
from our own awareness and concern.
In faith may we merely speak a word,
not lend our own. God only knows the
perfect plan, our finite minds distort at
every turn. But deep within the feelings
rise and truth is seen, each one his own,
then peace of mind begins.

E. Ann Berens

POETRY IN MOTION

Along the road one day
I saw a man in motion.
Garbage collection
was his occupation.

Jogging beside the truck
he set a rhythmic pace.
He'd stop, pick up a can
and swing it to the truck,

Each can was put beside
the curb, by ordinance observed.
Working in unison with him
the driver would keep pace.

With measured speed
he'd slowly grind along,
from house to house, taking
all refuse they could find.

Beauty was in this simple
dance, joy in the rhythm.
Each time the garbage truck went by,
we watched with fascination.

This man, with vivid imagination,
had raised his menial task each day
from dull routine to creative dance—
an artist was at play.

MORNING AFTER RAIN

Glow, glisten, gleam—steam
in the sun after rain. Clear, clean
air, still but for gentle breeze,
rustling damp leaves.

I stayed at home alone to
glory in this quiet scene.
My parched, stale spirit
struggling for space.

Groping for oneness with
my inner self, awed by a
neighbor's death, my love's
near brush with accident.

Too close to life, to death,
not standing back, detached
enough to see it clear, to
know I'm where I want to be.

Damp, rich earth relieved by rain.
Plants feeling earth against their
roots, regenerated, nurtured, fed—
and I—an integrated part of life again.

SECTION 5

BEING AWARE OF EVENTS AND HAPPENINGS

THE ROCK CONCERT

Appalling scene—of scattered shoes and clothing
strewn across the entrance to the Coliseum.
Bodies had been moved away—tragic victims of
fermented energy—lust for saturnalia of sound—
released by electronic beat.

The crowd had waited hours for the event.
Excitement charged the scene, impatience rose
as time crept slowly to the long awaited hour.
Then someone heard a practice melody.
This was enough to break their self control.

Led by the madness of a few, they forced
an entry through the doors. A crowd of twenty
thousand young, pushing, fighting all the way.
Wild egotistic power surged through their veins,
seizing them in frenzied fight.

Resolve to satisfy their greed became a frantic
struggle to survive. Some fell, and those immediately
behind, unable to hold back the thrashing mob, trampled
the people underfoot. They reached their goal not knowing
that their senseless drive had left eleven dead.

Collapsing in their ill-gained seats they calmed to the
hypnotic beat, focused in worship of the writhing stars,
some driven by an inner drive to fill their existential void,
some there for fun with friends, trapped in a perverted scene.
We all of us were there.

GUYANA TRAGEDY

All power comes from God—
let no man take that glory to himself,
only reflect it back to God.

Let no-one follow another blindly.
If self glorious, cease to follow him
for his path leads only to destruction.

A man who seeks the truth, questions
unceasingly, and lives with courage
by what he finds, is worthy to be followed.

May he remember those before him who
were loved and followed by those who
saw, in them, the greatness of their God.

GULF WAR

Poised on the knife edge of reality—
peace is the balance pole.
My mind knows peace, hold on to that.

Abyss—on either side—abyss.

Balance the power.
People play power games leaning
to chaos or to bliss, each side—abyss.

Tense times tick minutes by.
We watch and wait—
torn between love and hate.

Fear flames minds to paranoia,
caught from the precipice by a
sudden glimpse of sanity.

Step carefully each step, pray peace.
Tread lightly on taut line of truth.
Walk straight along the knife edge of reality.

Abyss—on either side—abyss.

ILLUSIONS

Is this war illusion—created by our fears?
Can we dispel the horrors with our prayers—
like dreams fading as we wake?

When we come to our senses
knowing what is, instead of what isn't,
do the nightmares disappear?

The Scuds are canceled by the Patriots—
like thoughts. We remain confused—torn
between our imaginings.

RESPONSE TO THE MILLION MAN MARCH

God bless Maud, Lord!
She called me today, her mind
enraged at Farrakan stirring
hatred in the hearts of black men.

She said—"It's love we need.
I love my friends—black ones, white ones,
Asians, Jews. I love them, one to one. Injustice
has been done it's true, but only love can heal"

Million Man March on Capitol Hill—
is not for hate. Fathers, sons, and brothers, friends
feel their pride, inside, take home renewed resolve
to be the sons and fathers that they are.

So far to come to prove you're somebody.
You knew that long before. No need atone,
alone, you are the man you're born to be.
Stand up with pride, you're free!

TENUOUS LIFE

How tenuous life is—a tight rope,
close to death, a needle's eye to thread.
Each moment lived, decision made,
opens to eternity. We are the
gatekeepers of our fate, for better
or for worse.

Three young, vibrant lives, with
seeming endless destiny, extinguished
in a flash, life's precious promise lost.
But who's to know that fate dealt them
a blow? Beyond this earthbound life
their spirits soar to join their source
of life, light, love—set free to be.

And we, who stay behind, struggle to
heal, to understand this tragic loss.
Weddings are rearranged, children are
born and joy is found again. Sorrows
are set aside but never gone.
How tenuous is life.

(Tragic death of John Kennedy and friends.)

THE PLAY

Energy focused on a point in time and place.

Imagination sparked one mind to gather
untried actors from all walks of life, fired by
vision of potential, faith in possibilities.

Infectious dream picked up the theme,
enthusiasm fused a team as each became
a tile in the mosaic of the art.

As time went by, like instruments, the actors
tuned, blended in pitch and harmony,
balanced in sound and energy.

My struggling memory, related line to line,
connecting cues. I leaned upon the fabric of support,
the trust and love, encouragement and hope.

We wove our garment, thread by many colored
thread into a warp and weft—the play. We blended
with each other in a subtle weave, achieving unity.

And in the final hour the people watched, were
moved, responding to a new dimension
of the Christmas scene.

Energy focused on a point in time and place.

(The play was "The Coming of Christ" by John Masefield.)

WEDDING

Culmination of a rich unfolding.
Two—awakened to each other,
aroused to dare to be themselves.

With sensitive intelligence, gently
persuading with the tenderness of
honest love, to dare to trust, be vulnerable,
let go the ancient screens shielding
their inner depths, so long protected
from all forms of hurt.

Beauty is now revealed in radiancy,
like the full bloom of flowers.
Loveliness of form, adorned exquisitely.
Each detail pondered to express this joyful
moment, to be long remembered.

A glimpse of glory like a flash of light,
celebration among many witnesses—
sharing the feast, the music, sounds of
friendship, focusing energy, bearing buoyantly.
Blessing the two, now one—abundant life,
new hope, new depths of love.

CELEBRATION

Larger than life—this scene—reverberating music,
people talking, walking, dancing, feasting.
Some dressed in Indian garb, gathered to celebrate
a marriage—two cultures merged in overwhelming love.

Blazing vision had seared his way through countless obstacles.
Two wheeled ride on rugged roads, through, isolated villages.
Hot nights, torrential rains, driven by a memory so strong,
a hope that could not, would not be destroyed.

Strong in her love she'd waited knowing he would come.
Clear in her vision of their destiny, her will tested by fire
and flood like tempered steel, had paved the path for his return.
No dangers daunted them. Glowing embers flamed to fire—a
blazing bliss.

Larger than life, it seems—this family, a microcosm of an
integrated world, passionately bonded as an entity.
Accepting each for what and who they are in their diversities
—caught in each other's joys.

Larger than life—they are.

THE WEDDING

A rich experience—gathering of friends
and family drawn from far and near, from
turning points in life—school, travel,
adventure.

And now to this once lonely place made
sacred by their love, friends came to celebrate
the merging of two lives. Blended family,
made complete: Pace, Tenne, Tia, Wendy, Keith.

The wedding sealed their vows, symbolic
rings exchanged encircling them in love.
Music, food, the wine and beer added
to the atmosphere.

A shadow play of eighteen years of love, of
heartbreak, crossing paths, going separate ways,
waiting until the time was ripe. Each time they
met, rekindled love, led to this wedding day.

Gradually the people left filled with new
hope for gladness in the world. Their
faith restored to claim their right to happiness.
And still the flowers bloom, and children play.

CHURCH FIRE

Black, charred, woodwork wrinkled unbelievably,
like a youthful face suddenly deformed.
New varnished wood transformed to hideous
mass, shapes retained, but beauty gone.

Memories of human scenes, of friendly talk,
concern for human plight, a place of warm
relationships, support and understanding—
here in this now darkened place.

Some came searching, lost, afraid, to find
they're not alone, others because of need
Tears fall in sadness now, grieving for their
home from home.

What smothered anger at humanity could vent
itself in such an act? What dammed the channels
of the flow of love in that one life, 'til it exploded in
this act of hate and violence?

And why? Do these doors seem closed to some?
Do we appear self satisfied, a group who set
ourselves apart, protected from a sick society?
So many questions to be answered.

GRADUATING

Beginning, ending, end, begin again—

The last stretch done—joy released
when stress gives way to sleep, rest,
time at last to talk, walk, play.
Shared struggle ends in victory for some;
sadness for those who still must work towards
the goal not quite achieved.
We all must know a little of what lies ahead.
Who will replace the bitter sweet with emptiness?

Beginning, ending, end, begin again—

The scene is different now. In all the struggle
to achieve the goal, did she forget the end,
the reason for it all? Did means become the end?
if so, not now. New obstacles stand in her path.
Challenges forcing her to search, to travel far
or near to find the work to meet her needs.
Courage to try, to fail and try again, perhaps
to compromise, and try a different path.

Beginning, ending, end, begin again—

Open mind—attempt a new approach.
What does she really want?
Where does she want to be?
She'll wait till she is sure, she'll act on what
seems right. She'll have the faith to follow leads.
She'll sometimes make mistakes. A door will
open here or there, and slowly, choice by careful
choice, she'll find her way.

Beginning, ending, end, begin again . . . .

SOME YEARS AGO

It was the morning of my older brother's
wedding day, the telephone rang—early to rise,
I answered it.

"May I speak with your father—I'm calling from
The Isle of Man."
My other brother Ken was there.

Fear held me tight. His love of racing
motor bikes had drawn him there,
he was to race that day.

My father took the phone. Low voiced
he talked, then went to my mother,
to tell her that her younger son was dead.

Her gut-felt wailing pierced the walls. How
could she face this day that was meant
for joy and celebration?

I took the news to Chris, Ken's fiancé, driving my car,
not knowing what I'd say. She let me in.
She'd had a dream of this. I couldn't stay.

The wedding was performed, too late to stop,
although the couple said they'd wait
until another day.

Somehow my mother made it through,
braving the scene, hiding her agony,
waiting to grieve, until the guests had left.

LOUD CLEAR MESSAGE

There's a loud, clear message coming through.
—a desperate cry, subconscious groan,
shown in furtive, semi-humorous talk of
ghastly acts, imagined, hinted at,
forgotten as unthinkable.

> "Listen to me, hear me, don't you understand?
> I speak, I warn, but you don't recognize
> the signs of danger in my cry for help!
> For God's sake take me seriously for once.
> I have the power, I can destroy, if that's
> the only way you'll notice me.
> Your heads are buried in the sand,
> filled with your schemes, your dreams,
> not minding me."

Sharp crack of bullets fired
across the room, shatter the chatter,
giving way to screams, ending dreams.
It happened in a flash—too late to stop
the damage done. A tragic hour.

There's a loud, clear message coming through,
deep from the human spirit starved, crying,
trying to be heard.

EAB

E. Ann Berens

THE FACE OF FEAR

I stand on the edge of terror.
Tears well in prophetic horror
of what may come.

Bulldozer keeps rolling on
and no one's stopping it.
In fear I watch not knowing why.

Do something someone—I cry.
Many know more than I
who are more qualified to try.

There must be something I can do.
I'll find some power within,
courage to stand my ground.

I'll say what I see, speak out,
not hide inside, pretending all
is well yet seething within.

This once brave country struggles
on the brink of change, battling
false security and facing fears.

It happened before and led to war,
I'll open my eyes, reveal the facts,
demand our liberty, equality for all.

Fear will not rule us here.
We can dispel the false—
proclaim what's true.

DESPAIR TO HOPE

There is fear across the land.
Faith in our leaders is shaken.
We are betrayed with lies.
Solid dams show signs of failing,
holding tons of water poised
above sleeping towns.

The fabric of our infrastructure
decays while we watch.
There is no money to fix it.
Ill-gotten wars bleed our country
of its young, its rich resources.
We're trapped in a vicious cycle of violence.

But something good is stirring.
A ground swell of unrest
rises from the grass roots up,
lifting apathy to action, searching
in desperation for a way to turn
the tide, to change direction.

People came out in droves to vote.
Some decide to take a stand
and do what's right—refuse
to rubber stamp the president,
cease to take a line of least defense,
they join to make a show of strength.

We will not wait while greed
and pride divide and seek
to overpower the weak.
The people's power is irresistible,
gathering momentum through the Internet
like a mighty wave breaking on shores.

THE HURRICANE

Infrastructure of the land
has broken down.
Leaders look to leaders
finding no one at the helm.

People wait for help in vain,
stranded in their broken homes.
They cling to what they know,
afraid to go.

Hurricane, earthquake, storm
or fire, bring out the best
in some, who know instinctively
what they can do to overcome.

They push their way through
obstacles that melt before their stare.
They see despair and dare to answer
prayer to bring relief and care.

And we who stay at home, afraid
to leave our comfort zone,
perhaps maintain a backdrop of
stability, a calm somewhere.

No one is left untouched by such
a tragedy, so many devastated lives.
Our gifts, so small a sacrifice, change
us from our complacency.

It seems each one of us must
stand alone, take action as we can,
prepare for what may come—
and be responsible.

THE PILOT

Totally focused on the challenge of the now,
he did what he was trained to do
as geese struck violently against the plane.

Split second choices cleared his mind.
All other thoughts shut out.
Survival was his only task.

Passengers and crew obeyed each call,
catching the force of each command,
selected carefully.

They listened, heard, braced for the shock
they knew would come, transfixed with fear,
held close by this commanding voice.

Tail down, wings level as they struck the
rivers edge and glided to a stop.
Chutes deployed, they left the plane.

Shocked into silence—no one screamed.
Calm of the pilot's voice had held them all
and led them to the safety of the floating wings.

They stood and waited for the boats, the floats,
all of them saved. Intense concentration kept
the pilot focused on his task.

He did what he was trained to do.

SECTION 6

BEING ALIVE

DANCER

Proudly the dancer glides across
the path with poise and grace.
Her feet push lightly at the ground, her
body flows like batter poured upon itself.

Her hips continuously move, shaking
the ornaments around her waist,
adding their music to the sound
of zills that chatter in her hand.

Her body sways, her undulating arms,
twisting seductively, keep flowing as she
trails her scarf. Her hair flies freely 'til
the Eastern music ends and she is still.

EAB

E. Ann Berens

CLIMBING FREE

Naked they chose the challenge
of the rock, far from the culture
comforts of their homes.

Entranced by mountain majesty,
its awe inspiring power, they test
their skills, their spirits, on life's
cutting edge, with strength, resources
that they did not know they had.

Poised in ultimate responsibility,
they face reality, their truth, identity.
An instant flash of knowing perfect
peace of mind, exquisite oneness
with the Universe.

TOO MUCH

Heal whole, wholly. Lie limply, let go.
Two in a row—too much,

Too sudden to lose—loved horse so
quickly gone, soft muzzle remembered
nickering your hand, hot breath warming
your heart. Gone now to Elysian fields,
leaving you lost awhile—mourning your
horse, your dog, too much too soon.

Lie limp, let go, the fever too will pass,
drain your body of its grief, give time
to heal whole, wholly.

Cool hands, smooth brow, wipe clean
of stress, leaving a tender peace like
fresh breeze cooling the night.

Lie limp—heal whole, wholly.

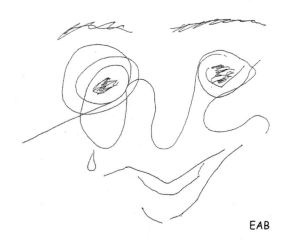

EAB

E. Ann Berens

PROMISE OF SPRING

Cut grass smell—fresh, green,
like a meal—intoxicates with Spring.
Pruning fruit trees—climbing
through branches, lost in a maze
of twigs, cutting for light, air, space,
making room for bloom.

Pulling weeds—freeing smothered,
last year's mothered, plants.
Hands in rich brown earth—
harbor of minute life, nurturer of seeds.
The smell is clean and rich
promising life and growth.

Visions of color blaze through
my mind—enriching. I'll plant a mass
of flowers—yellow, blue and purple, red—
against green privet hedge. Flowering
rosemary will creep over concrete
walls covering blankness with soft touch.

Nasturtiums, radiating brilliant flame
amid lush leaves, will lend a pungent scent.
The vision fades—bare patched lawn
from drought surviving, yellow daffodils
amid deep grass. Predominance of green,
and the heady smell of Spring.

A PLACE TO CONTEMPLATE

Fresh green glade set back
from the road—beauty of
flowers, trees and rich new
grass in gracious space.

Each time I pass
I glance at it with awe.
There is a mystery
I can't explain.

Six months ago
a house stood there,
always with several beat up
cars against the road.

Once when my car had broken down,
I'd stopped and asked to use their phone.
They'd kindly let me in. Gratefully
I made the call and left.

Now—no trace of human living stays.
Illusions pass, reality remains.

WAITING

Alone and waiting for the 'plane,
hopes rising, excitement welling,
yet bridled with the fear of disappointment.

The void will soon be filled,
loneliness replaced, a feeling of
completeness soon restored.

The missed companionship, laughter
shared, unanswered questions unresolved,
dilemmas pondered.

And then at last, the 'plane arrives.
But did he get another flight? Excitement
mixed with apprehension keeps the moment tense.

Then he appears. Opposing feelings burst with
relief at sight of the familiar face, he walks toward
me—happiness to share.

HOME COMFORT

Cats curled by the glowing fire, absorbing warmth,
watching the glow, flickering colors, sparks
rising from crackling logs.

Coolness of the evening gone, we sit in comfort
the day's work done. Worries of tomorrow
not yet considered, we talk, we rest, read,
gather thoughts and look them over,

Shelter of home, of treasured things, the
curved glass cabinet, the desk my grandmother
wrote at. What thoughts have circled round? What
feelings were expressed upon the surface of this
desk? What indentations left from trembling pen?

Do feelings linger, keeping a flow of spirit
moving, merging past with present?
Do impressions made on old and much used
furniture absorb emotions, thoughts?
Surrounded by familiar things, I feed my
psychic needs from them.

This contact with the past, helps make me whole—
leading to the future.
Beneath the surface a whole new world exists,
we cannot see or feel or touch it, only be aware.
Perhaps beneath the material veneer lies a
deeper level of life.

E. Ann Berens

THE TANGLED WEB

I free you from my tangled
web of anxious thoughts,
to soar to heights and depths
beyond my ken, to pierce
through avenues that are not
mine to know, but yours.

Yours are the thoughts, ideas,
encompassing your mind.
My path pursued will lead me
far if I will let yours go.
What arrogance I had to worry so,
as you continued on your way.

Paths will converge from time to time
we'll share our anguish, sorrows, joys.
We'll comfort each other, understand,
then go our separate ways, strengthened,
released, respecting each the other's
inner self to lead the way.

STEWARDS OF THE EARTH

I am here. I am as God created me.
God is within me and surrounds me,
in everything I see, hear, touch.

The moon-bright heavens inspire with their
magnificence. Dazzling waters reflect the
glory of the sun or gloomy darkness of storm clouds.

Trees, flowers, grasses host all kinds of life
lushly covering fertile land. Deserts stretch
far, reminding me my vulnerability.

This fragile earth, in all its careful balance,
commands respect from all who dwell on it,
from microscopic life to human beings like us.

Each has its part to play within the universal plan.
Beware the powerful few who rape and devastate
the earth for selfish gain.

We cannot know the interplay that keeps earth whole.
We'll trust Earth's order, harmony and health to God's
Creative Energy that permeates all life.

SURFER

Raging surf, screaming wind,
teaming life—challenge for the soul.

Intimate knowledge learned on the surf
close to the wave, skimming the sea.

Perception gleaned, excitement—
close to fear, thrills the senses.
Each wave rolls in demanding action,
movement now, or tumbling powerless
in the crashing sea, caught by this
frightening force, learning signs of
the surf—being one with the sea.

God—how we dream, how we hope,
how we build our lives, our reality.
May we meet each challenge
courageously, and face each fear
as we surge with the waves,
blow with the wind and flow
with the tide—in life's sea.

MELODY

This garden is a melody
of bloom and shades of green,
a tranquil scene.

Pink peonies have opened
in the last few days, leaning
over driftwood to the sun.

Siberian iris grace the rocks,
their gentle blue lure bees
from trees.

Flaming poppies stand near evergreen.
Sunburst locust trees play host to most.
Black squirrels leap while songbirds sing.

Lush rhubarb leaves soak up the sun
near compost heap. Birdbath, sundial,
trellis, fence provide defense.

E. Ann Berens

EDGE OF BEYOND

Crashing seas—ceaseless motion.
Swelling, sinking, wearing stone, grinding sand,
eroding rocks—un-harnessed power.

Seaweed, driftwood, sea-birds, fish,
shells and colored stones,
environment of freedom, space.

Pelicans gliding stately by
then dropping like stones
to make their catch,

Seagulls crying ceaselessly—that
mournful, eerie cry. Each intent
upon the purpose of their inner drive.

Sand and pebbled shore washed clean each tide,
left virgin smooth, sandpipers' footprints gone.
Continuing cycle along the edge of beyond.

DROPS OF WATER

Single drops of rain fall on earth's
parched, dry crust breaking up hard
impenetrable lumps.

Saturated, they crumble, leveling the earth,
speeding change, soaking fertile seeds—
wind blown or dropped by passing birds.

Rain becomes a storm, replenishing lakes,
and seas, swells banks of rivers flowing
faster than before.

Rising waters threaten lives and towns'
defenses until the storm subsides.
Water flows—meeting the needs of all.

CHANGES

So many changes happen in life.
Nothing remains the same. Conditions,
alter, adjustments must be made.

A tree is pruned, new buds emerge.
All life is motion. Tall trees bend in the
wind, their roots cling deep within the soil.

A man decides to build a house. Digging
deep, he questions the soundness of the rocks.
And when he's sure he builds with confidence.

He travels far for answers sure, settles only
for the truth, taking time to reach his goal,
he acts with faith in his beliefs, trusting himself.

Strong foundations hold the framework of his
home, despite the winds, the storms that drive
with force upon its walls.

REALITY

God is—
Deep, shared Nucleus of the Universe,
stable Center of us all. Core of Truth,
—All that is.

God is—
Around, within my inner depths,
reflection veiled by clouds of limitations
learned from thoughts of death and separation.
Fear upon fear forms fog of self deception.

God is—
Though threat of war blinds bliss, wastes vision,
shatters trust. So easily my mind gives way to
morbid images. Nightmares flash through fickle mind
fanning fear to flame.

God is—
Remembered—instant flash of joy returns the memory.
Even a loving smile transcends the horrors in my mind,
as eye meets understanding eye, bridging the
self-made gap.

God is—
Love—Truth—sole Reality—
Focus for sanity—Peace—
God is!

E. Ann Berens

TEARS

Tears—overflow of feelings,
joy and sadness, internal suffering
or overwhelming gladness.

Tears—washing away the fog
that hides a painful memory,
healing the strain.

Tears, re-living joyful memories,
like forgotten flowers
revived by rain.

Tears—evidence of empathy, the
human leveler, dissolving pride.
Admission of oneness with humanity.

OPEN TO LIFE

Malignant cells transformed—

    translucent bubbles freed
    into the atmosphere,
    floating harmlessly
    until they burst—
    sprinkled to eternity.

Illusions of fear, despair,
evaporate, like a forgotten dream.

    Funnels spew foam like
    fountains of froth disgorged
    into the sea lost in dilution,
    their fount, now emptied,
    filled with blessed light.

Nightmares dissolve, dispersed
by golden radiance. Wellspring redeemed.

(Written for Nancy McCay who recovered from cancer through prayer, spiritual nurturing and faith as well as radical medical treatment).

E. Ann Berens

THOUGHTS ON THE UNIVERSE

Bubbles converge and burst
breaking fine film that separates
what is within.

So do our individual lives, each
in its micro world, merge, converge,
as one pulsating energy.

Meeting of minds reveal connections.
Randomly discovered coincidences
speak of the macrocosm.

We cannot know the whole, our unique
purposes are all to each of us until we
catch a glimpse of how we all are one.

Bubbles converge and burst
as one complete reality.

CURVES

Curve of water over rocks—making waterfalls,
catching sunlight, sparkling, reflecting light.

The perfect curve of crescent moon
lending light to midnight sky among the galaxies.

Curves of human form—the beauty of young eyes,
warm breasts promising gentleness and perfect peace.

Curve of waves beckoning surfers to risk
oneness with the sea, curling towards the shore.

Roads curve allowing smooth, continuous flow
at speed, no break to change direction.

Curve of sails catching wind to carry yachts
across wide waters, yawing constantly.

Some day a perfect curve, continuing in open
space, may find completion in full circle.

Is that the final learning curve?

E. Ann Berens

TREE SEED

Tree seed dropped in fertile soil,
grow straight and tall.
Born for greatness, beauty,
long life and stateliness.

Seedling, blown by winds, made strong
by storms, learning to stand alone.
Blazing sun shines down—nurturing,
goodness, released from the soil.

Young tree—stretching to catch the rays,
roots reaching deep into the soil,
open to the elements, unafraid,
serene in cosmic harmony.

Full grown tree—its full potential realized,
providing shelter, shade. A thing of
beauty, grace, tranquility,
symbol of permanence, stability.

INDIVIDUALITY

My mind is a molten mix of metaphors,
like bubbling lava as it merges to volcanic
edge, creeping relentlessly to overflow.
What is this drive to build infernos in my
mind, a kind of tension, self imposed anxiety?

I need some time alone each day, when
thoughts can flow like water in a stream,
tumbling easily whichever way they will,
sparkling in a glorious effervescent flood,
following channels of their own.

Peace can be found, maintained, a constant
balance must prevail between my needs and yours.
So, can we dance a give and take, a synchronicity
of alternating steps, advance, retreat, swing to
the beat, repeat to meet again?

In mutual serendipity we can create a symphony
of sound giving each other room to move, create our
individuality, penetrate a wall to truth, mining gems
of poetry, ideas of creativity. Together we can follow
each our separate way. This is our challenge for each day.

E. Ann Berens

SHASTA

Black whisper of love—
gentle, fragile, stepping lightly,
featherly to settle on my breast
while I lie waking at dawn.
Soft rub of fur on my chin
she caresses me.

But not for long—she loves
us both. Adoring cat—quietly
she moves across the bed
linking us both, unsure of
where she wants to be and
then she settles in between.

She'll leap to my shoulder—
no need for claws to hold her place,
her eye ball measurement is true
she seems intent on gentleness.
I've never known a cat like her, like
a breath of air, a whisper of love.

COLORS

Blues and greens of skies and forest
growth, of seas, lakes, rivers, surging
waters rushing by, reflecting deep blue
sky amid green fathomless depths.

Yellow-green of frogs and grasses merge
to turquoise, jades of every shade, to
dark blue-green of somber pines.

Pinks, blues, purples intermingled
in a single bloom, catch my eye to
wonder at their beauty.

Reds, browns, yellows—rich colors
of autumn days, warm senses
in the cooling season.

As flames leap in glowing hearth
igniting logs, burning orange, green
and purple gasses radiating heat to
warm the heart.

So energy continues—from sight
and sound of beauty, stirring emotions,
passing the stream of life forever on
encircling the universe.

All creation glories in its flow.

THE STEPS

The steps we built beside the house with
redwood forms and concrete poured and
stone washed pebbles bare, we use with pride.

Before, a steep rough slope with grooves
served as a pathway to complete the
circuit of the house.

Now there is no path too difficult to tread
around our home, no hesitation marks our step.
Forgotten are the days when it was steep.

Along its side red cyclamens grow among
the rocks, and none would know that it
had not been there for long.

Each feature added to our home draws
our roots still deeper into the soil
of the home we own.

FAITH ALIVE

The building stretched between two roads—
brick upon brick behind a cloistered way, spire
reaching up as if for strength toward the sky.
Green lawn and rhododendrons draw the eye.

This church, symbol of strength and permanence,
rebuilt from devastating fires, provides stability
among confusion in the world—merging time
and space with ageless faith.

A focal point converging human energy for good,
enduing those who choose with inner strength
to act, react, to care, to share—centered on love
and truth, involved in the community.

This church—a body of diverse souls, repeatedly
attuned to God with thankful, open hearts, fired
by a vision for society—a world made right through
Christ's revealing of the truth.

(The First Congregational Church of Berkeley, CA. U.S.A.)

HOMELESSNESS

Hope seed—
Planted in fertile soil
of searching soul,
brought near despair
by desperate circumstance.

Hope seed—
Fed by courage found to save from
devastating doom. Mother, father,
other, finding supernatural strength
in spite of overwhelming odds.

Hope seed—
Spark perceived in dark, near
hopelessness, breathed into
enduring flame by every hint
of care, dispelling fear, leading to light.

Hope seed—
Blooming into flower—the vine
moves imperceptibly from unseen
source, inch by inching into full,
abundant life.

CREATIVE ENERGY

Could it be that man is an extension
of God who made us?
Why do we imagine ourselves apart,
separate from the creative start?
Why would it leave us?

A sculptor molds a figure, expressing
creative force within, part of himself.
Are we not vessels of the same creative
power, outpoured beyond ourselves
—the lives we live?

Christ made it clear he was a man.
"God is in me and I in Him" he said.
Do we complicate the mystery?
Can we not see it in simplicity?
Why do we separate humanity?

We're part of a whole, bound one with another,
expressing different sides of God.
If we believe it—we acknowledge Him.
God is in us and we in him. This understanding
opens up a whole new world.

E. Ann Berens

BEHOLD THE MAN

Quietly, firmly he stood before the men who had
been led to him. He did not try to hide, to run away.
He'd faced the awful fear before this day.

Just as a sailing boat slows without wind, so did his
foes stop in their tracks. They were not used to men
accused, who'd stand before them unafraid.

Crowded with men and arms the aggressors backed,
bewildered, thoroughly defused. How to arrest a man
who won't resist, that was their question now,
until their problem was dispelled.

When Peter burst his bounds and struck an accuser's
ear, with sword from scabbard wrenched—this act
dispersed the tension building up in each man's breast.
The soldiers now could deal with this.

Here was a natural man whose deeds they could predict.
They were no longer seized with fear. Peace was restored-
Jesus would not allow an act of violence to set off
a chain reaction now.

So he was bound and, at his wish, his friends were allowed
to go. All through that day and night the questions came.
He answered straight with fact. At no time did he fail to
face reality. Even when struck he answered truthfully.

He reached the governor finally who questioned him again.
Tired though he was his will was still at ease. But Pilate
could not understand a man so unafraid, who, knowing
what would come to pass would still proclaim the truth.

SECTION 7

GLIMPSES OF BEING

GLORIOUS MORNING

God—It's beautiful!
Early morning sun shines on tree tops—
gift of promise, joy.

Distant waters mirror blue, their
storm churned waters transformed.

Hill follows hill—gently curved
like breasts nippled with trees.

Sunlight beckons buds,
brings out the brilliant greens
of new growth.

Tender points of new life pierce
rain softened earth, vulnerable
like a new born babe open to life.

God—Let me not spoil this bliss.

RENEWAL

Emerging from the center of the
tattered mother plant—
a new green point of tight furled
leaf pierces the air.

E. Ann Berens

THE SOURCE OF LIFE

Attached to the vine the branches
reach like streamlets from a
mighty river passing living water
to all who drink.

Close to the Source of Life we stay,
renewed again, our frailty strengthened,
pouring balm of hope and joy on all who
suffer and in suffering grow.

NOW

The here and now, this is reality—
the precious present.

The past is gone, now it is history.
The future is to come.

Our present choices determine its
events, holding its consequences.

Focus each moment, live each hour,
regenerate vitality in living.

FIRST RAIN

They were dancing in the first rain
of the season, like children gleefully
at play, frolicking close by their
stately parents feet.

Three young eucalyptus trees, just six
feet tall, cavorting with a joy to be
alive, singing in the wind and rain—
shimmering in all directions at one time,
like "wheat fields and Cypress",
whitish green leaves caught the light—
constantly moving.

WIND

The wind blows on.
It whirls, hurling
leaves across the path,
bending trees, pruning,
leaving them stronger,
healthier. Their
roots respond to
force of the elements.
Trees bow and sway,
not resisting all the way,
but moving with the wind.

OUR AILING EARTH

We are the tool of our own destruction.
We interfere with, only God knows what.
Forgive us Earth our arrogance to
think we understand the total
interplay of all created things.

How can we dare to turn the tides
and now arrest the domino effect
of what we've set in motion?
Is it too late to save our ailing Earth?
Are we past the point of no return?

BLOSSOM

Blazing blossom catches my eye—
like the glare of snow surprising
the morning.

Blazing blossom—fed by loved
pets buried below, coursing
Earth's elements—from life
to death to life again.

REAL

Clinging to the Earth, anchoring
to something solid, what is real anyhow?
Flashes of life come and go, I try to catch
some meaning in it all, for me. I grasp a
project, work on it, create something
to give or keep. I cling to what I've
made to make me real.

GIVING

To give, I must let go,
release the gift.
To hope for thanks, to
watch, to wait, to wonder
if the gift is used, is loved—
is not to give.

Giving is love expressed.
The gift is but the symbol.
Two people—flash of joy,
a flush of gratitude—the
gift, a bridge, a bond
between the two.

AIRPORT

Wide polished corridors
open to sky roads,
scattered with people
in limbo, in transit—
coming, going, waiting,
sleeping, passing time,
watching planes landing.
Thoughts where they're
going or where they've
been, not here, not
now, but then.

Airport—a limbo land
between realities.

CONNECTING

Some people know where you're coming
from, looking deep in your eyes they know.

Eye meets eye—searching,
reading the hopes, hurts, fears.
Why does that touch me to tears?

Meeting of minds, all kinds, crossing
through boundaries, reaching your core,
barely known any more.

Eye meets eye like lasers sealing,
healing connections. Essence meets
essence like liquids blending.

FRIENDSHIP

Senses harmonized, minds attune,
like swallows swooping parallel,
joined by invisible thread.

Friendship is born when thoughts
converge in one shared moment like
streamlets funneled down a waterfall.

Flash of insight, like a photograph
of focused sight, touches heart
and mind in common understanding.

Friendship is born.

CHILDREN PLAYING

Children playing on concrete,
softened by their rubber wheeled bikes.
Playing for freedom from their fears, the
hardness of their lives in the crowded city.

Being children in an adult world of push and pull,
trying to make sense of who and what they are,
making sense out of chaos, responding
to occasional grass and lilacs.

CAT COMFORT

Black cat on my lap, encircled by
my loving arm, safe in my aura,
absorbing what she will of me, I
finding comfort from her softness.

Closed circuit of love, enjoyment
of peaceful interchange, touch
on velvet fur, releasing tenderness
in me, delighting in each other.

ECLIPSE

Soft, muted light, not the glare
of usual days. The world seems quiet
today, hushed land. We watched
reflected pin hole image of the sun,
guarding our precious eyes, fascinated
by the sight, while scientists captured
treasured data through their telescopes.
Not for another hundred years or
so will Earth view this eclipse.
What will we be then?

HUMMING BIRD

Humming bird bright,
gem-like bird. Energy
poised, vibrating wings,
holding still in air.

Feeding, hovering,
darting, as if intention
is enough—it is there
where it wants to be.

It is, immediately.
Instant movement from
flower to flower, to tree, flying free.

DEER

Still, standing,
aware, alert,
listening among trees.
Head turns toward me,
watching. It moves
placing each step carefully.
Suddenly it leaps,
bounds away,
springing through
brush, free to
come, to go.

SWAN

Curved white neck
against blue water,
gliding gracefully.
Calm, tranquility. Purity
and peace, perfect form,
poised in space, focused
energy, majestic sight,
lifting, raising hope,
shining light on a moment.

Edwards Brothers, Inc.
Thorofare, NJ USA
August 11, 2011